INVESTIGATING UFOS

Heinemann Library
Chicago, Illinois

PAUL MASON

© 2004 Heinemann Library
a division of Reed Elsevier Inc.
Chicago, Illinois

Customer Service 888-454-2279
Visit our website at www.heinemannlibrary.com

Originated by Ambassador Litho Ltd
Printed and bound in China by South China
Printing Company Limited

08 07 06
10 9 8 7 6 5 4 3 2

**Library of Congress Cataloging-in-
Publication Data**
Mason, Paul, 1967-
   Investigating UFOs / Paul Mason.
      p. cm. -- (Forensic files)
Summary: Examines some famous cases involving
UFOs and describes how
forensic science can sometimes be used to
explain such events.
Includes bibliographical references and index.
   ISBN 1-4034-4834-5 (lib. bdg. : hardcover) --
ISBN 1-4034-5474-4
(pbk.)
   1. Unidentified flying objects--Juvenile
literature. 2.
Investigations--Juvenile literature. [1.
Unidentified flying objects.]
I. Title. II. Series.
   TL789.2.M36 2003
   001.942--dc22
                                    2003018160

Acknowledgments
The author and publisher are grateful to
the following for permission to reproduce
photographs:
pp. 5, 8, 9, 12, 16 Fortean Picture Library; p. 6
Charles Walker/Topham; p. 7 Paul Villa/Fortean
Picture Library; p. 10 USAF/Cowin Collection;
pp. 13, 20 Robert Harding Picture Library; pp.
14, 22 Klaus Aarsleff/Fortean Picture Library;
p. 19 Frank Spooner Pictures/Gamma; p. 23
OSF; p. 24 Hulton Archive; pp. 26, 28, 33, 38
Mary Evans Picture Library; p. 30 CUFO; p. 31
Sandro Vannini/Corbis; p. 34 Michael Buhler/
Mary Evans Library; p. 35 Topham Picturepoint;
pp. 36, 39 Bruce Maccabee; p. 40 National
UFO Reporting Center; p. 42 Travel Ink.

Cover photograph of a flying saucer reproduced
with permission of Imagebank/Getty Images.

Some words appear in bold, **like
this.** You can find out what they
mean by looking in the glossary.

Contents

UFO Investigations

July 1999: a telephone rings in an ordinary house in an ordinary street somewhere in Florida. A man goes to answer it. He listens carefully, asking a few short questions now and then. Finally he says, "I'll be with you in 40 minutes" and puts the receiver down. He picks up his keys and a small bag containing a camera and a tape recorder, plus some paper for making notes, and heads out the door.

A sighting

Several people have seen a UFO near a small coastal town. A bright red light suddenly began hovering in the sky about a mile out to sea just after dark. One man ran inside to get a camera and managed to take a photo before the light disappeared. The film will be developed tomorrow, and may provide **evidence** of what the **witnesses** claim to have seen. In the meantime, the **investigator** starts to interview people, taking notes and recording what they remember. Three of the witnesses describe the same thing: a bright red light out to sea. A fourth witness thinks the light was orange, and started over land before moving out across the ocean. A fifth witness says the same thing, but adds that the UFO seemed to drift back and forth before disappearing.

What is the mystery object? What it could be is a UFO. UFO stands for Unidentified Flying Object. However, many people now associate UFOs with visitors from **outer space.** Early UFO sightings seemed impossible to explain using the technology of the time: UFOs appeared to do things that nothing on Earth could, so people thought that they must have come from another world. Whether visitors from outer space are piloting these particular red lights is not yet certain.

A birthday balloon

Jump forward one month: August 1999. The **investigation** is complete, and the UFO was definitely not a **hoax.** But it was not a visitor from outer space either. The photo taken by one of the witnesses has been examined: it does show an orange-red object hovering out to sea. The distance is hard to tell because the photo is a little blurry. The object could be almost anything, but what it actually turns out to be is a Chinese lantern. On the night of the sighting, a birthday party was taking place outdoors half a mile away. The lanterns that had been used to light the party had birthday balloons filled with helium (a gas lighter than air) attached to them. One of the lanterns had become loose and was pulled up into the sky on the breeze. It drifted out over the sea before finally going out.

This picture was reported to show UFOs over Italy in 1954. In fact, the picture is a **fake** photograph taken by a press photographer.

Modern UFO fever was sparked by Kenneth Arnold's sighting in 1947 of a string of what became known as "flying saucers." Arnold actually used the word "saucer" in his description of how the UFOs flew, saying: "They flew like a saucer would if you skipped it on the water." But the word stuck as a description of their shape, and many of the UFOs sighted over the coming decades were apparently saucer-shaped.

Modern investigation

Today, UFOs are a big business. Thousands of UFO magazines and books are printed in many countries and there are hundreds of UFO websites. There are plenty of reasons for someone to invent a claim that they have seen, or even been aboard, a UFO. They might want the fame, to get their picture in the paper, for example. Or they might want to make money, selling their photos of UFOs and articles about their experiences. A modern UFO **investigator's** first job is to try and sort out "real" sightings from **fake** ones.

This distant shot is **alleged** to show a UFO in the skies above Stiermark, Austria. in 1971.

Some people genuinely believe they have seen a UFO but are mistaken. An investigator's second job is to decide whether the "real" sighting is of a craft visiting Earth from another planet, or something that can be

Investigator's toolbox

A UFO investigator's toolbox includes:

- **Witness** <u>accounts:</u> do the witnesses all agree on the details? If there is only one witness, does he or she have any reason for making it up?

- <u>Photographic evidence:</u> many photos are obvious fakes—they have been tampered with, or the object in them is not a UFO. Photo **analysis** includes checking that a UFO is not an everyday object viewed from an odd angle, and the distance of the object from the camera.

- <u>Physical evidence:</u> is there any physical **evidence** of a UFO? For example, is there crushed vegetation at the landing site? Is there evidence of radiation, or traces of other **residue** from an **alien** craft? Is there anything strange about the person who has apparently been aboard a UFO, such as unexplained marks on their body?

Occam's Razor

William of Occam was an English philosopher who introduced "Occam's Razor." This rule states that the simplest, most obvious explanation for something is the most likely to be true.

Often, using Occam's Razor leads to a logical explanation of UFO sightings. For example, someone who sees lights in the sky might think he or she has seen a UFO. But if he or she lives near an airport, the simplest **theory** is that they have actually seen an airplane.

The First UFO

Date: June 24, 1947
Location: Pendleton Airfield, Oregon

A large crowd has gathered to wait for the arrival of a small airplane being flown by Kenneth Arnold. Arnold is a former football star, but that is not why the crowd is waiting to see him. Word has reached Pendleton Airfield that Arnold has seen nine objects flying in a "screwy" formation at an incredible speed. Arnold later remembered that when he saw the objects "I took my map from its snap holder, grabbed a ruler, and began figuring miles per hour. I thought my figures were wrong and that I had better wait until I landed at Pendleton to do some serious calculating."

Arnold's story

Kenneth Arnold was an experienced pilot. He worked selling and maintaining fire-control equipment. Because of the distances he had to travel, Arnold used a light airplane to get from place to place.

On June 24, Arnold was flying back from Chehalis Air Service in Washington, stopping at Yakima (also in Washington), before finishing his journey at Pendleton in Oregon. On the first leg of his journey Arnold passed close to Mount Rainier, near where a U.S. Marine Corps transport plane was thought to have crashed. There was a $5,000 reward for anyone who spotted the crashed plane, so Arnold was keeping a careful eye on his surroundings.

Kenneth Arnold's strange experiences sparked off the first modern UFO craze.

It was at this point that he spotted the group of nine unidentified flying objects. These objects were later to become famous as the modern world's first UFOs. At first Arnold thought it was just a flight of geese. But they were moving too fast, given how far away they seemed to be. They could not be geese—but what were they?

By Kenneth Arnold & Ray Palmer

Arnold later described what he had seen in a book titled *The Coming of the Saucers*. He was also interviewed by the *Oregon Journal* on June 27, and said the objects were, "flat like a pie pan and somewhat bat-shaped . . ."

Arnold's 1952 book, *The Coming of the Saucers*, described his UFO encounters.

Air force planes

Today, some people have claimed that what Kenneth Arnold saw that day were new experimental U.S. Air Force planes being tested in remote Washington. Modern-day **investigators** have suggested two possibilities based on what is now known about experimental planes being developed at the time:

1. The tail-less "flying wing" planes designed by Jack Northrop, an aircraft designer whose planes first flew in 1947. The planes certainly looked similar to the sketches Arnold made of what he had seen. However, only one of these had been built at the time, and it had been grounded by mechanical problems since the previous September. The second Northrop plane made its first flight two days after Arnold saw the "flying saucers."

2. The Ho IX plane, similar to Northrop's design, was to be based on a frame brought back from Germany at the end of World War II. However, there is no record of even this one frame ever having been built into an aircraft, let alone nine of them being made.

Speed Calculations

The main thing that established the strangeness of what Arnold had seen was the speed at which the objects were traveling. At one point, he had thought they might be military planes. Interested in how fast they could fly, he tried to calculate their speed. Arnold had seen the objects fly between Mount Rainier and Mount Adams in 1 minute and 42 seconds. Estimating how far they were from him, he was able to use his own position to work out their speed.

Arnold's calculation of speed was based on the **altitude** of the objects, which he said was "9,200 feet [2,800 meters], plus or minus 1,000 feet [305 meters]." Arnold saw the UFOs pass behind a sub-peak of Mount Rainier, which he knew to be a certain distance away—it was the only peak high enough to get in the way of him and the objects. This is why he knew how far away they were. Knowing their distance from him, plus the time it had taken them to cover the distance between Mount Rainier and Mount Adams, he was able to work out their speed.

Jack Northrop's XB-35 "flying wing" plane looked similar to Arnold's drawings of the UFOs he saw.

When Arnold got to Pendleton his figures were checked and found to be correct, though they seemed incredible. The saucers had been flying at around 1,200 miles per hour (1,900 kilometers per hour): twice as fast as the U.S. Air Force's fastest jet of the time. People found it alarming that there was something in America's skies that could go twice as fast as America's best fighter planes. Journalists got hold of the story, and word began to spread across the country of Arnold's "flying saucers."

t seemed there were only two possible explanations for these strange craft. One possibility was that the **USSR** had developed an aircraft far better than anything the U.S. could produce. This seemed unlikely—at the end of World War II two years before, **Soviet** aircraft had not been as good as American ones. The second possibility was that the UFOs came from **outer space.** People believed the second explanation and so the world's first UFO craze began.

But what if Arnold had miscalculated the speed of the UFOs he saw? If that were so, the explanation for what he saw might be found on Earth, rather than outer space.

Possible errors

Arnold's calculations of speed were based on the distance between him and the UFOs he saw, which he calculated as being 27 to 28 miles (44 to 45 kilometers). He thought that this was the case because the objects passed behind a sub-peak of Mount Rainier. But it is possible that he miscalculated the distance, and therefore the speed.

Arnold said that the UFOs had "disappeared from sight behind a projection on Mount Rainier on a snowfield." But a group of white or very light-colored objects could easily have disappeared from sight in "front" of the snowfield, rather than behind it. If this had been the case, and the objects had passed in front of the sub-peak, there would be no way to be sure how far the UFOs were from Arnold's position, and no way to work out their speed.

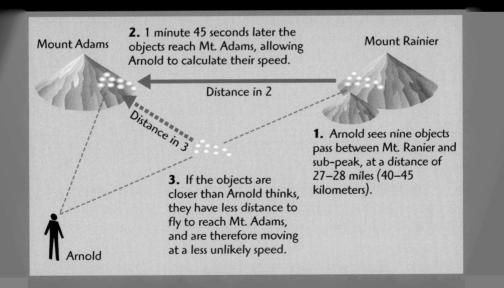

Mount Adams

2. 1 minute 45 seconds later the objects reach Mt. Adams, allowing Arnold to calculate their speed.

Mount Rainier

Distance in 2

Distance in 3

1. Arnold sees nine objects pass between Mt. Ranier and sub-peak, at a distance of 27–28 miles (40–45 kilometers).

3. If the objects are closer than Arnold thinks, they have less distance to fly to reach Mt. Adams, and are therefore moving at a less unlikely speed.

Arnold

A likely explanation

On June 25, 1947, in an interview with a local radio station, KWRC, Arnold gave details of what he had seen. These details would, 50 years later, prove crucial in suggesting a likely answer to his UFO mystery.

Modern-day **investigators** of Arnold's UFO sighting have several facts available to them. The source for these facts is Arnold himself. He was undoubtedly an honest man, though possibly a mistaken one. Below are the basic facts of Arnold's description of what he saw:

Kenneth Arnold holds a picture of what his UFO would have looked like from above. Arnold only saw the objects at a distance and from the side.

• The objects he saw flew in a strange way, dipping and rising as they moved along. As well as comparing them to skipping saucers, he said they looked like "the tail of a Chinese kite."

• The objects were only seen clearly when the sun flashed on them, and they had black wingtips.

• The objects looked like a pie plate cut in half, with a triangle sticking out of the back.

• The UFOs were seen in Washington, near the Cascade Mountains, at a high **altitude.**

Armed with this information, an answer to the riddle of what Kenneth Arnold saw on June 24, 1947, can be found a lot closer to home than **outer space.** It now seems almost certain that what he saw was not flying saucers from another **galaxy:** instead it was a flight of American white pelicans. In fact, the press first suggested this idea. A newspaper told of an airline pilot who had seen "nine big round disks weaving northward . . . We investigated and found they were real all right: real pelicans." The answer was there all along, but no one was ready to believe it.

UFO or American white pelican? Arnold probably saw a group of pelicans like the one pictured here, with the sun shining brightly off their white feathers.

Arnold never admitted that the objects were birds. In fact, he had a similar encounter five days later with what he initially thought was a flight of ducks. He dismissed this idea because "ducks don't fly that fast," when in fact ducks have been clocked at airspeeds of up to 75 miles per hour (120 kilometers per hour). But he did say that "they had the same flight characteristics as the large objects I had observed on June 24."

Flying saucers or white pelicans?

American white pelicans can weigh up to 33 pounds (15 kilograms) and have a wingspan of 10 feet (3 meters). But how do investigators think Kenneth Arnold could have mistaken pelicans for flying saucers?

Even today pelicans are spotted **migrating** across the Cascade Mountains at high altitudes, but they are rare and Arnold may well not have seen them before. The white underwings of the pelicans can reflect light off a snowfield, ice, or water, so that they flash in the sunlight just as Arnold described. The movement of pelicans through the air, alternately flapping and gliding, is exactly like the "skipping" motion Arnold described. Finally, pelicans have black wingtips, just as Arnold described.

Date: July 8, 1947

Location: Roswell, New Mexico

Today's front-page story in the local newspaper, the *Roswell Daily Record*, is a startling one for many Americans. "The intelligence office . . . at Roswell army air force base announced at noon today that the field has come into possession of a flying saucer." The saucer had apparently crashed on land belonging to a local rancher, and pieces of the **wreckage** had been collected by the air force for examination. Coming so soon after Kenneth Arnold sighted nine UFOs in Washington (on June 24, 1947), this new event filled people with panic. Was the United States about to be invaded or attacked from the air?

UFO or weather balloon?

This is a picture of the site near Roswell, New Mexico, where a mysterious "UFO" crashed in July 1947.

The UFO wreckage had actually first been spotted some days earlier, on June 14. Ranch foreman Mac Brazel had been doing his rounds late in the afternoon when he spotted a line of **debris** about seven miles (eleven kilometers) from the ranch house. In a rush to get his chores done before dark, he assumed it was the wreckage of a weather balloon—a balloon launched to measure the weather conditions at particular **altitudes.** Weather balloons had crashed on the ranch twice before, so it was natural for Brazel to think this

Nothing more came of the sighting until Brazel went to the nearby town of Corona days later. He heard about the Arnold UFO sighting, which had sparked a rash of UFO reports across the U.S. UFOs had been reported in 39 different states. Brazel began to wonder about the wreckage he had spotted several days ago. After thinking about it, it seemed to him that there had been far more debris spaced over a wider area than with the previous weather balloon crashes.

On July 4, 1947, Brazel went back to the crash site with his wife and daughter. He collected some pieces of the wreckage, and two days later drove into Roswell with them to show the sheriff. The sheriff called the army air base and spoke to **intelligence officer** Major Jesse Marcel. Marcel later remembered thinking that "a downed aircraft of some unusual sort might be involved." He and Captain Sheridan Cavitt headed out to the ranch to examine the wreckage themselves.

Disputed statement

The press release from the air base announcing the recovery of a flying saucer has been a source of argument.

On the day the report was sent out, the base commander, Colonel Blanchard, was away on leave. It is unclear who **authorized** the press release. Intelligence officer Major Marcel is quoted in it, but claimed in 1979 not to have authorized it. Marcel says that information officer Walter Haut wrote the release without permission. Haut said in 1995, "I honestly cannot remember whether I wrote it. How the colonel passed that information on to me I cannot honestly tell you."

Arguments like this one are common throughout the Roswell story—people remember things differently, and sometimes remember something completely different. This makes sorting out the truth of what happened extremely tricky.

Weird wreckage

Marcel's son, Jesse Junior, was eleven years old at the time of the Roswell UFO crash. He remembers that his father woke him and his mother one night, wanting to show them "something about flying saucers." Marcel spread **debris** across the kitchen floor. His son remembered there being "black, brittle plastic material that had either melted or burned, and a lot of metal foil." Also in the **wreckage** was a beam of something as light as **balsa wood,** with strange violet images on it. Major Marcel felt that these images could be some sort of **alien** writing. He packed up the wreckage and drove back to the air base with it.

Over the years since the Roswell UFO crash, many claims have been made about what materials were found among the wreckage. It has been claimed that the wreckage was extraordinarily light and tough, as light as balsa wood but impossible to break. It could not be cut, or even scratched, using a pocket knife. Apparently, despite several attempts to set it on fire, it would not burn, and some pieces of wreckage were made of what appeared to be tin foil. But when it was crushed and rolled up, the "tin foil" unfolded itself into exactly the shape it had previously held, with no signs of creasing. It could not be torn.

Other stories suggest that the air force recovered almost an entire spaceship, and has been trying to hush it up ever since. Certainly the day after the "flying saucer" story was released, the air force denied it was true. They claimed that what had been discovered was in fact a crashed weather balloon.

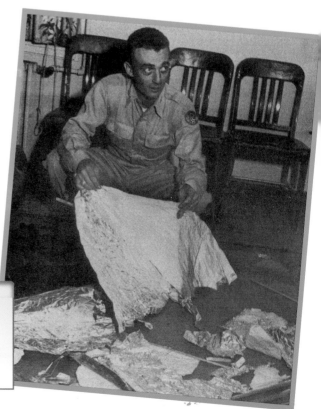

Major Jesse Marcel of the U.S. Air Force is shown here holding wreckage from the UFO.

16

The **atmosphere** at the time was feverish. People were seeing UFOs everywhere. Some worried that the **USSR** had developed **nuclear** technology and was using it to power terrifying new aircraft. Others thought that aliens were planning to invade Earth. Rumors of something mysterious at Roswell continued to emerge. Today, some people even **allege** that the bodies of small aliens were recovered from the wreckage of the craft. The bodies were then taken to Roswell air base, before being smuggled elsewhere in children's coffins that were ordered specially for the purpose.

False allegations

Many of the allegations made about the events at Roswell seem likely to be false.

- The wreckage contained mysterious materials, including tin foil fabric that kept its shape, and could not be torn.

Untrue: Major Marcel's son, who was one of the first to see the **evidence,** says: "I didn't see that."

- Major Marcel removed alien bodies from the spacecraft.

Untrue: Even Marcel said that this was false, and denied ever seeing any bodies.

- The bodies of small aliens were transported from Roswell air base in coffins designed for human children.

Untrue: Officers from the base are said to have moved whiskey and other drinks in coffins, to stop the liquor from being stolen while in transit.

Finally, an answer

The answer to the question of what did crash near Roswell in 1947 has slowly begun to emerge. Just as some people have **alleged,** the U.S. government did attempt to cover up the truth about the mysterious events. But they were not trying to keep a captured **alien** UFO secret. Instead, they were hiding the truth about an unidentified flying object of their own: Project Mogul.

Project Mogul

The U.S. government finally released information on Project Mogul in an attempt to put an end to Roswell speculation. So what was Project Mogul, and why was it so secret? The answer lies in the international rivalry that began after the end of World War II. The U.S. at this time had **nuclear** bombs; the world's other superpower, the **USSR,** did not. The thing American military planners feared most was that the USSR would develop its own nuclear weapons, and use them to attack the United States. What the U.S. needed was a **device** that could tell whether its enemies were testing their own nuclear weapons.

Project Mogul was a device made to listen for the faint echoes of a nuclear bomb being exploded. It consisted of a 650-foot (200-meter) long train of 23 weather balloons each 13 feet (4 meters) across. The device carried **radar reflectors,** special microphones to listen for giant explosions, battery packs, pressure switches, and other devices. To prevent its discovery by the USSR, only top-ranked officers and politicians who needed to know of its existence would ever hear about it.

Crash landing

Mogul Flight 4 left Alamogordo military airfield, southwest of Roswell, on June 4, 1947. It rapidly gained height and drifted northeast. As some of the balloons burst, Flight 4 began to sink back to Earth, finally coming to rest at a ranch near Roswell managed by Mac Brazel. As the balloons reached the ground they continued to be blown along by the wind, dragging radar reflectors and other equipment behind them. It was this **debris** that Brazel saw on June 14, and then took to Roswell for examination.

The staff at Roswell air base had no knowledge of Mogul Flight 4. They did not immediately recognize the **wreckage** for what it was. One of the two officers who were first to see it, Captain Cavitt, did think it was some sort of weather balloon, but Major Marcel was the senior officer and was unconvinced.

The air force knew what had really crashed, but could not tell anyone because it was a top-secret project. Instead of telling the truth, officials covered up the issue with half-truths that did not explain the full facts. Without a proper explanation, people were able to make up **theories** of their own to fit the facts they had heard. At the time, with UFO sightings happening every week, a crashed UFO was the explanation many people felt best fitted the facts.

This **faked** photo allegedly shows an alien from the Roswell crash. Nonetheless, some people still claim that the bodies of aliens were removed from the wreckage.

The Nazca Spaceport

Date: 1950s
Location: Nazca Plain, Peru, South America
A single jeep appears from the haze of the desert. It heads for a small mound and stops. A woman emerges and takes out a 10-foot (3-meter) stepladder, which she climbs armed only with a notepad, then begins to write and sketch. What is the woman—whose name is Maria Reiche—drawing? In twenty years the most popular **theory** will be that it is an ancient **spaceport**, used by visitors from other **galaxies.**

How could people without aircraft have made these lines? Some writers have argued that they must have been helped by **extraterrestrials.**

The Nazca Plain

Seen from the air, the things Maria Reiche was plotting become clear. The Nazca Plain is covered in straight lines. Some are parallel tracks, while other lines intersect. From the air, some lines are drawings of animals and birds, including a 445-foot (135-meter) long condor. The lines were made by the Nazca people, who lived in the area from roughly 200 B.C.E. to C.E. 600. They had scraped away the rocky top layer of soil to reveal the different-colored ground that lay beneath, then edged the lines with rocks. Since the drawings are visible only from the air, and it would be another 1,500 years or more before aircraft were invented, the lines are a mystery. How did the Nazca people make them?

During the 1960s and 1970s, a writer named Erich von Däniken suggested that the Nazca lines had an extraterrestrial use:

> seen from the air, the clear-cut impression that the 37-mile [60-kilometer] long plain of Nazca made on me was that of an airfield!

Von Däniken also claimed that the likely explanation for the lines was that:

> at some time in the past, unknown intelligences [**aliens**] . . . built an improvised airfield for their spacecraft which were to operate in the vicinity of the Earth.

The books in which von Däniken explained his ideas became very popular, and the idea of a spaceport in the Peruvian desert took hold of many people's imaginations.

Alternative explanations

One of the foundations of von Däniken's theories about an ancient spaceport was that the drawings could be seen only from the air. They could therefore have served as "signals" that had been "built according to instructions from an aircraft." In fact, modern **investigators** have suggested that there are other possible explanations.

In 1982, investigator Joe Nickell and five assistants set out to reproduce the giant condor drawing in eastern Kentucky. Both sticks and string would have been available to the Nazca people without alien assistance. So, Nickell and his team used only these in their attempt to recreate the condor. They used a grid system to enlarge a small drawing, making each square from the drawing many times bigger on the ground. The end result was a perfect copy of the Nazca condor.

An answer in the skies?

Maria Reiche, a German-American mathematician and amateur archaeologist, who spent her whole life mapping and investigating the Nazca lines, did not accept the spaceport theory. She pointed out that von Däniken's "runways" were on soft ground, and joked, "I'm afraid the spacemen would have gotten stuck" in the soft soil.

Other **investigators** have made a different objection: would space vehicles that were able to travel across **galaxies** need runways miles long? It seemed more likely that they would be able to land vertically. Yes, replied supporters of the spaceport idea, but perhaps the exhausts of hovering spacecraft had actually made the "landing strips?" Unfortunately, this idea is even less likely than the **alien** visitors needing long runways. It is not the area's light soil that has been cleared to make the lines and drawings; it is the heavier rocks that are laid alongside the cleared ground.

This is a picture of Erich von Däniken, the **controversial** writer whose **theories** about the Nazca plain have helped sell tens of thousands of copies of his books.

A sky map

The likely explanation for the Nazca lines was discovered by accident. Dr. Paul Kosok of Long Island University in New York was working in the region, studying ancient irrigation (artificial watering) systems. He noticed that on the winter solstice, the shortest day of the year, one of the main lines pointed directly at the point on the horizon where the sun set. Other lines match different points on the calendar.

Modern computer techniques have allowed investigators to recreate the night skies of 1,500 years ago, when the lines were made. Some of the animal and bird shapes on the plain seem likely to match the positions of stars in the sky at the time the Nazca people lived on the plain. When viewed from the raised mounds, from which several of the lines flow, many of the lines also line up with the positions stars occupied at that time. Scientific **investigation** has shown that the Nazca lines are almost certainly some kind of map of the skies.

Computer history

One of the techniques used to test likely answers to the Nazca mystery is the use of specially designed computer programs. Earth shifts the angle of its **axis** very slightly each year, so the stars always appear in a different part of the sky. Stars also disappear, and new ones appear, through the centuries. From one year to the next the difference is hard to spot, but over thousands of years the night sky can drastically change its appearance.

Investigators are now able to program computers to determine what the night sky was like between 200 B.C.E. and C.E. 600, when the Nazca lines were made. Using this information they can assess whether the lines had a link with the stars.

This giant condor from the Nazca plain was reproduced in Kentucky using just a small sketch, sticks of wood, and lengths of string.

UFOs in Space

Astronaut Jim McDivitt reports seeing a UFO during Gemini 4, an early NASA space mission. "While we were in drifting flight, I noticed an object out the front window of the spacecraft. It appeared to be **cylindrical** in shape . . . From one end protruded a long, cylindrical pole with the approximate fineness of a pencil. I had no idea what the size was or what the distance to the object was."

Astronauts' sightings

UFO magazines and websites often carry stories about astronauts having spotted **extraterrestrial** craft during their missions. One of the most popular and oldest stories is that of Neil Armstrong, the first man to walk on the Moon. He saw two "other spacecraft" on the surface. Armstrong has never confirmed saying this. Other stories say that the astronauts who went to the Moon saw **alien** bases and mining operations there and were warned not to come back.

There are many more rumors about UFO sightings by astronauts. Some astronauts are said to have seen tiny, snowflake-type objects overtaking their space capsules. In one instance, two astronauts are reported to have seen four UFOs linked together, traveling in a convoy. In another, an astronaut is supposed to have spotted a flying saucer.

Unfortunately for UFO **investigators,** there are usually simple explanations for the real identities of the objects that are **alleged** to have been UFOs. And in many cases the stories about astronauts spotting UFOs have simply been made up. Most often the UFO turns out to be a **satellite,** a piece of the astronaut's own spacecraft that has been **jettisoned,** or ice crystals that have come off their spaceship.

Here John Glenn climbs aboard his capsule, about to become the first American to orbit Earth.

Astronaut sightings: the truth!

- February 20, 1962: John Glenn, the first American to orbit Earth, sees three objects follow him, then overtake his Mercury capsule.

True: Glenn did see these objects, which he said were very small, like "snowflakes." Many other astronauts after him also saw such objects, and were able to make them appear by banging on the sides of their capsules.

- Mercury VII; May 24, 1962: astronaut Scott Carpenter takes a photo of a flying saucer.

Untrue: Carpenter took a photo of a tracking balloon that had just been ejected from his capsule. Distorted by the glass of his window, it looked slightly oval in shape.

- Gemini 4; June 3, 1965: astronaut Jim McDivitt spots a cylindrical UFO.

Untrue: McDivitt did not recognize part of his own rocket that had been jettisoned. His eyes were red and bleary after contact with chemicals during an accident on board.

- Vokshod 2; March 8, 1965: Russian cosmonauts are said to have seen a cylindrical object while in orbit.

True: They assumed it was just a **satellite,** almost certainly correctly.

- Gemini XII; November 11, 1966: astronauts Jim Lovell and Buzz Aldrin see four UFOs linked together.

Untrue: The objects were not unidentified—they were four bags of garbage the astronauts had ejected about an hour before.

Date: September 3, 1965, 1:00 A.M.
Location: Route 150 near Kensington, New Hampshire
Norman Muscarello is making his way home to Exeter, having been to see his girlfriend in Amesbury. Muscarello has been hitchhiking, but for the moment the road is quiet and he has to walk. Suddenly, as the road rises up Shaw's Hill, a mysterious object appears in the sky nearby. It is football-shaped, with bright red lights along the side that light up the surrounding area. "I'm all alone," he remembered later, "I just froze up. I didn't know quite what to do. I got scared."

A second witness

Muscarello's encounter had not been the first sighting of a UFO that night. About 30 minutes earlier, Officer E. F. Bertrand of the Exeter Police Department had stopped to investigate a car parked by the side of the road. In it he found a woman who told an incredible story—so incredible that Bertrand did not believe it at first. She said that she had been chased for twelve miles (twenty kilometers) along Route 101 by a mysterious object flying through the air. She described it as being roughly cigar-shaped and surrounded by a "halo" of red lights. The UFO had swooped at her car several times, before shooting off as she left the road.

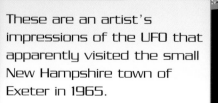

These are an artist's impressions of the UFO that apparently visited the small New Hampshire town of Exeter in 1965.

Officer Bertrand stayed with the woman for about fifteen minutes, and then returned to his patrol duties. He was amazed to get a message from the police station saying that Muscarello had just appeared there, looking very agitated and describing his encounter at Shaw's Hill. Bertrand immediately headed back to the station to speak with Muscarello. There he heard the story of what had happened to him.

The UFO had floated in a wobbling, silent motion toward Muscarello, who said later that he thought it was about 80 feet (25 meters) wide. It came so near that he got scared and hid behind a low wall. The UFO then began to hover over a nearby house, bathing it in red light: "the whole side of the building seemed to turn out like a blood red." He watched until the UFO moved away from the house, then ran and knocked on the door. There was no answer, so he continued along Route 150 until he was able to flag down a car and get a ride to the police station. Together, he and Officer Bertrand decided to go back to the area where the UFO had appeared.

Radioactive tests

Scientific **investigators** from Pease air force base near Portsmouth, New Hampshire, looked into the Exeter incident. The tests were carried out at the air force base because the U.S. Air Force had responsibility for investigating potential threats to U.S. aerial security, including UFOs.

Among the tests they conducted were searches for any sign of **radioactivity** in the area, the most advanced form of **propulsion** scientists could imagine at the time. They hoped to come up with some explanation of what had powered the mysterious craft, and therefore **evidence** that it had been there, but the tests came up blank.

A police witness

It was 3 A.M. by the time Muscarello and Bertrand arrived back at Shaw's Hill. They got out of the police car and began to walk across a field. At first they saw nothing unusual, but then suddenly dogs nearby began to bark and horses to whinny. Muscarello shouted a warning, and Bertrand turned to see the UFO rise up silently from behind a pair of pine trees.

Both men were startled; some newspaper reports say that Officer Bertrand drew his gun to defend them. They ran back to the police car, and Bertrand sent a radio message back to headquarters: "I see the damn thing myself!"

Moments later another police car arrived on the scene. Its driver, Officer D. R. Hunt, had heard the message and came to investigate. The three men sat watching the UFO move in the sky for about ten minutes. They later said that its light was incredibly bright— so bright that it was painful to look at directly. The lights along the side would pulse in a repeating pattern, rather than being on at all times. The UFO zipped around the sky, moving from place to place faster than their eyes could follow. Finally it moved to the southeast.

Norman Muscarello is shown here in 1965, not long after he and Police Officer Bertrand had encountered the spaceship.

A mysterious call

Another aspect of the incident at Exeter concerns a mysterious call to the telephone operator at Hampton, a nearby town. She took a call from a man desperate to be put through to the police.

He told her that he had been chased by a "flying saucer"—just as the female driver who had first sighted the UFO had been. Before the man could identify himself or say where he was calling from, the line went dead.

What is fascinating about the Exeter case is that two of the **witnesses** were police officers. They had no reason to lie, and in fact could have lost their jobs if they were discovered not to be telling the truth. As a result, the events surrounding the UFO sighting at Exeter have fascinated people ever since.

Natural explanations?

Several "scientific" possibilities from the natural world have been suggested to explain the mysterious events in Exeter, including:

- ball lightning: somehow stimulated by the high-power cables that hung near by. This seems unlikely because ball lightning is normally less than 20 inches (50 centimeters) across, lasts just a few seconds, and occurs mainly during thunderstorms.

- St Elmo's Fire: a brightly visible leap of electricity from objects in contact with the ground to the air. It leaps from points such as telephone poles, ship masts, and radio antennas. But the brilliant lights in Exeter moved along, rather than hovering above a particular spot such as a telephone pole.

- "corona discharge:" a bright light that occurs near high-tension power lines in very rare circumstances. However, this requires the discharge of very high levels of electricity, which would have had to come from the local system. Engineers from the Exeter and Hampton Power Company did not report any power losses that night.

FILE CLOSED

Date: July 26, 1975, 3 P.M.
Location: Zwischbergen, Switzerland
Three Dutch hikers have stopped for a rest very close to the little
Swiss village of Zwischbergen, not far from the popular ski resort
of Saas Fee. Suddenly they are astounded to see a circular object
hovering in the air above them, 330–1,640 feet (100–500
meters) away. One of them manages to snap a quick photo of
the UFO before it glides behind some trees and disappears.

Worldwide evidence?

Copies of the photo were seen around the world. William H. Spaulding,
a UFO photoanalyst, examined the photo in 1977. He said that the UFO
was about "25 to 30 feet [7 to 9 meters] in **diameter**" and was moving
toward the camera when the photo had been taken.

This is a close-up of one of
the **controversial** photos
taken near Saas Fee.

Eight years later
another photo of a
UFO emerged from
Zwischbergen. On
careful examination, this
"UFO" turned out to be almost certainly a picture of a bird.
This prompted **investigators** to look again at the Saas Fee photo,
to make sure it was genuine.

New **analysis** of the photo suggested that the UFO might have been
close to the camera, not far away as originally thought. It turned out t
throwing an aluminum camping plate through the air like a Frisbee m
it possible to take an almost identical photo. Far from being the best
photo ever taken, the Saas Fee photo seems likely to be a **fake**

The mountains around Zwischbergen have become notorious for UFO sightings.

Photo analysis

Photo analysis is one of the tools available to UFO investigators in deciding whether a sighting is genuine. Two analyses were made of the Saas Fee photo, with different results.

W. H. Spaulding's 1977 analysis of the Saas Fee photo included an important error. Spaulding analyzed only a third- or fourth-generation print of the original slide. This meant that it was a copy of a copy of a copy of the original. With each copy, the quality of a print gets worse, so Spaulding was working from a very inaccurate version of the photo.

The later analysis of the photo suggested that the dark-colored area at the bottom of the UFO had not been distorted by distance. If it had been, the edges of the dark area would be less defined than they appear to be. The object was therefore probably quite close to the camera.

The Garden Grove Abduction

Date: 1975

Location: Garden Grove, California

In a series of eight weekly hypnosis sessions, a 33-year-old man known only as BS tells a horrifying story. He tells Dr. W. C. McCall that **aliens** have **abducted** him several times. His incredible tale— of experiments on humans, **tractor beams,** colonies of **clones,** and a "mind" called the "Host" that controls others—is backed up with such incredible detail that McCall and professor Alvin H. Lawson are convinced he is telling the truth.

Taken by aliens

BS tells the doctor that in 1971 he had been camping with a friend in the Arizona desert. Suddenly they were caught up in a weird beam, which slowly lifted them up into the belly of a UFO that hovered overhead. Once aboard, two of the aliens grabbed BS and floated off with him down a long, curving hallway to a brightly lit room.

The aliens went to work at **consoles** in the room, while BS stood against a wall. BS was subjected to a medical examination that left him terrified. Next he saw a new alien, this one 9 feet (2.7 meters) tall, coming toward him. It stank and had bad breath, but when the alien touched his head he felt immediately calm. He was taken on a tour of the ship and he saw a vast laboratory, where creatures were created in test tubes. The things being born were clones made to serve the Host. This controlling intelligence took the form of both a giant computer and a fetal (unborn) being. BS was taken back down to where his friend was waiting. They were dressed, and then beamed down to the desert floor.

Taken again!

The revelations were not over yet. Before the seventh weekly hypnosis session, BS disappeared. He turned up 24 hours later, unshaven and dopey and dressed only in his pants. Under hypnosis he claimed to have been abducted once more and taken to Peru. There he had undergone a ritual with the aliens at the site of the famous spider on the Nazca Plain in South America. BS also claimed that he had first been abducted at the age of sixteen, and had been forced by the aliens to get a spider tattoo.

Impossible details

BS's story appeared fantastical, but it was backed up by details that it seemed impossible he could know. Though uneducated, he was able to provide detailed plans of the layout of the UFO that abducted him. Facts about the UFO's **propulsion** system contained **chemical formulas** using the **atomic weights** of different elements, to four decimal places. BS provided texts that had been written in a computer-like alien language, as well as a short message in ancient Greek from 3,500 years ago: "Nous laos hikano." This he translated as meaning "I come in the mind of man."

These aliens are shown here kidnapping humans in order to experiment on them.

This illustration shows more "typical"-looking aliens than on the previous page. Again they are experimenting on humans, who appear powerless to resist.

Then, suddenly, BS's story began to unravel. He claimed to have found a spider figure drawn in the dirt at the site of an **alleged** UFO **abduction.** But a young boy came forward to say that he had seen BS scratching the spider in the ground. Dr. McCall and Professor Lawson at last decided to check into BS's background. A series of disturbing facts emerged:

- BS worked for a computer manufacturer, which explained how he had come up with details to support the **"alien** computer" idea
- at work he was able to read books in the technical library—books that contained details of the **atomic weights** of chemical elements
- he had access to books by Erich von Däniken, about the idea that space aliens used the Nazca Plain in Peru as a space landing site
- one of BS's friends studied ancient Greek
- BS had said there were other **witnesses** to two of the abductions, but neither supported his story
- BS had already served time in prison for fraud (deceiving people).

In the face of all these facts it became clear that, as Professor Lawson later wrote, BS had "made monkeys out of us for a while." He had never been abducted by aliens, nor visited one of their space ships. He had, in fact, made the whole thing up.

Birth memories hypothesis

One of the explanations for why some people make up alien abduction stories is called the birth memories hypothesis. Psychiatrists can have people recreate the experience of being born using **hallucinogenic** drugs; other people recreate it under hypnosis.

Investigators have realized that many of the elements of these re-creations are similar to accounts of alien abductions. Many abductees claim that they squeeze through a small entrance into a large room. Others recall going through a passageway into a large, bright room at the end. Some abductees use very clear comparisons to the process of being born—one said that she had to twist her shoulders through 90 degrees to fit through the doorway; just as babies rotate while being born.

Researchers have suggested that abduction stories are a subconscious, or even conscious, fantasy that uses deeply buried memories of the process of being born.

This woman is showing a drawing of the alien she claims abducted her.

Gulf Breeze

FILE OPEN

Date: November 11, 1987

Location: Gulf Breeze, Florida

Edward Walters glances out of his window at the night sky and sees an unusual glow behind some nearby trees. Grabbing a camera, he rushes outside just in time to snap a few photos of a UFO heading toward his house. Moments later he is struck by a beam of light that paralyzes him. Walters struggles against the beam, which he thinks is attempting to abduct him, while a voice in his head keeps telling him to "calm down." He continues to fight the paralysis, however, and as an airplane flies by, the beam goes out. Moments later the UFO disappears.

Fame for Gulf Breeze

After a discussion with his family, Walters decided to send his photos anonymously to the local paper, the *Sentinel*. They appeared on November 19, eight days after the attempted **abduction.** Within a few months, the small town of Gulf Breeze had become a world-famous UFO-spotting location. There were hundreds of UFO sightings, many of them by more than one **witness.** People claimed to have seen UFOs being chased by jets, and to have been the victims of further abduction attempts. Local residents even set up a system to watch for UFOs.

This photo appears to show a low-flying UFO, one of many reported sightings from Gulf Breeze.

Different UFOs

Several different kinds of UFO were spotted around Gulf Breeze. One was a light that moved through the sky within about an hour of sunset. Usually the light started red, then turned white and began to flash. Sometimes it dropped other, smaller lights beneath it before going out. Often these red lights appeared in pairs, and they became known as "bubbas." Bubba is Florida regional slang for "brother."

Then, in September 1991, a new kind of UFO appeared. The UFO consisted of a ring of white lights arranged in an octagonal (eight-sided) shape. People saw the rings of lights on various dates; sometimes they were seen by large groups of people. The lights would move around the sky. The area at the center appeared to be several feet in **diameter.** The distance of the objects was difficult to judge at night, which made it tricky to work out their size.

Were the bubbas flares?

At the time of the bubba UFO sightings, it was suggested that the red lights were in fact ordinary road **flares.** To the naked eye, they seemed to be very similar in color. **Investigation** suggested that this was not the case. The UFO lights simply appeared in the sky, rather than drifting upward as a lit flare attached to a balloon might do. The optical spectrum of a flare was compared to that of a bubba. Measuring the optical spectrum—the exact kind of light an object gives out or reflects—is a scientific way of deciding the exact color of an object. A special screen was placed over the lens of a camera, which was then used to take photos of both a bubba and a flare. The screen showed that the bubba sent out more blue light than a flare. The scientists concluded that bubbas were not flares.

True or false evidence?

One of the most remarkable sightings of all was, just like the first, witnessed by Edward Walters. He was sitting at his desk on January 12, 1994, when he saw a UFO in the sky over Gulf Breeze. Grabbing a nearby camera, he began to take photos of the object.

As he took photos, Walters heard the noise of jets approaching. He saw two aircraft coming from the east, heading toward the UFO. One of the jets curved around the UFO and then continued west with its partner. Suddenly the jets turned back, heading for the UFO once more. Walters said that the UFO zoomed off to the east ahead of the jets, before turning south and disappearing.

Edward Walters is the man at the center of many of the Gulf Breeze UFO events. Some **investigators** are convinced Walters is a hoaxer.

Photos as proof!

One of Walter's photographs shows one of the jets passing in front of the UFO. From this, the size of the UFO can be calculated fairly accurately. The photo seems to suggest that the UFO must have been about 20 feet (6 meters) high and 40 feet (12 meters) across.

Many of the UFO sightings were by Edward Walters, which initially led to claims that he made the whole thing up. But many of the other UFO **witnesses** saw the same things, suggesting that Walters could not have made up the stories. There was also photographic **evidence.** Could there be an explanation other than **extraterrestrials** visiting Earth?

One explanation

Slowly, a possible answer to what caused the UFOs above Gulf Breeze has begun to emerge. A science writer named Ronald Schaeffer has investigated the Gulf Breeze events and suggests that they are a **hoax** by Edward Walters as a way of making money. Walters' three books on the UFOs, plus the payments for using his many photos, have made him a wealthy man. But other evidence has also come to light:

- A local youth claims that he, Walters' son, and another boy helped to **fake** the UFO photos.
- People who moved into a house Walters had lived in discovered a model of a UFO hidden in the attic of the garage. The model was wrapped in an old house plan drawn by Walters, suggesting that he placed it there. Using this model, news photographers were able to reproduce many of the original photos.

The Gulf Breeze case is not closed. However, there are still people who believe the area was, and still is, visited by genuine UFOs.

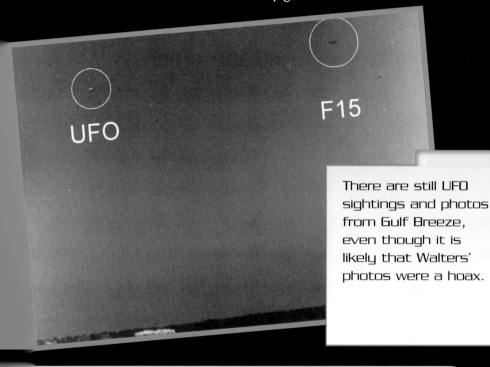

UFO

F15

There are still UFO sightings and photos from Gulf Breeze, even though it is likely that Walters' photos were a hoax.

Distance analysis

Edward Walters' photos of a UFO and an F15 jet close to one another have been analyzed to show the likely size of the UFO. Using the maximum possible zoom on Walters' camera, and knowing the size of the jet, it is possible to work out how far away from him the jet was when the photo was taken. It is also possible to calculate roughly the UFO's size, since it appears behind the jet.

The Phoenix Lights

Date: March 13, 1997
Location: Henderson, Nevada

At roughly 6:55 P.M. a young man in Henderson was amazed to look up into the night sky and see a large UFO overhead. He later described it as being about "the size of a [Boeing] 747" jet, and said that it traveled almost soundlessly, making a noise like "rushing wind." The UFO was V-shaped and had six large lights along its front edge. This was the first of probably thousands of sightings of UFOs that night. This string of events is now known as the Phoenix Lights, because they were centered on the city of Phoenix, Arizona.

Here is an example of the distinctive V-shaped lights seen above Nevada and Arizona.

Hundreds of sightings

The next sighting was by a police officer who, just after 10:15 P.M., saw a group of five lights, one trailing the others. The lights flew soundlessly away to the south, and disappeared over the skyline after a couple of minutes. Soon after this a rash of sightings occurred, with hundreds of telephone calls received at police stations, news organizations, and the nearby Luke air force base. The sightings included:

- three **witnesses** who saw a huge wedge-shaped UFO with five lights glide overhead
- a mother and her four daughters, who saw a giant V-shaped UFO hovering above them for about five minutes

- two air traffic controllers at Sky Harbor airport who reportedly saw the same UFO, as did several pilots
- a former airline pilot in the town of Scottsdale who saw the UFO pass above as it headed south of Phoenix
- UFO reports were also made in the towns of Glendale and Gilbert.

Two months later Luke air force base announced that it had investigated the sightings by interviewing witnesses, and could explain what people had seen. The lights had in fact been **flares** dropped over a firing range by an A-10 "Warthog" plane at roughly 10 P.M. This explanation, though, fell short of satisfying everyone. The sightings of giant UFOs by hundreds of people do not seem to be explained by a set of flares.

But is the air force's unsatisfactory explanation a clue to the real nature of the objects? Some observers have noted that the air force is trying to explain away events, even though their explanation seems obviously inadequate. Could they be involved in a cover-up of their own activities, similar to the one that sparked the Roswell **controversy?**

Calculating size

Many of the witnesses who saw UFOs on the night of March 13, 1997, emphasize the giant size of the objects they saw. One of the sightings was by a family of five people, who were driving from Tucson to Phoenix on Interstate 10.

They spotted the UFO while traveling at around 80 miles (130 kilometers) per hour. The UFO was moving in the opposite direction and passed overhead. They could see one of its two wingtips out of either side of the car. Using a line from their eyes to the edge of the car roof and on to the wingtips, they had a rough idea of its width. The object took at least a minute to pass them.

Even if the UFO was hovering instead of moving, and even if they were traveling at only 60 miles (100 kilometers) per hour, this would make the UFO at least 3,280 feet (1,000 meters) in length.

Journal du Vallée headline, April 23, 2004:
<u>UFO Alert Above Chamonix</u>

A UFO has been reported in the Chamonix Valley, a popular outdoor-sports venue that people visit for *parapente* (using a parachute-based **device** to fly from mountaintops), mountaineering, and other adventure sports. The sighting is the first in the valley, high in the French Alps, and was reported by two friends climbing together on the Mont Blanc **massif.**

A strange whistling

The two **witnesses,** Jean-Pierre Ribierre and Arnaud Bertrand, were climbing just below the summit (highest peak) of Mont Blanc when they heard a whistling noise from over the next ridge, sounding "like the passing of a giant wing." The two mountaineers moved toward the ridge to investigate.

Many people have reported strange experiences while up in the thin oxygen of the mountains.

Whatever had made the noise seemed to have disappeared. But then they suddenly noticed two bright flashing lights some distance away. "They were over toward the little village of Argentiére, about four miles [six kilometers] up the valley," he said, "and they zipped in and out of sight behind two peaks. I couldn't see their shape because of the brightness of

A French air force spokesman said that there were no training flights through the valley that day. "We have no explanation for what these men apparently witnessed, but I'd be surprised if it turns out to be visitors from **outer space!**"

What did the climbers see?

Here are some of the things you need to determine before trying to solve the mystery:

- The Chamonix Valley is a popular tourist destination, visited by thousands of people everyday. There would have been lots of people around when the UFO was spotted, but no one else came forward to say they had seen it.

- The valley is a popular destination for bird-watchers.

- There is a *parapente* launching site on the side of Mont Blanc.

- The two friends who saw the UFO have known each other since childhood, and have just begun to work together in a mountain guiding business. They have never reported a UFO sighting before, or been accused of any sort of dishonesty.

- There were no airplanes in the valley that day.

What's the answer to the mystery? What did the climbers see?

ANSWERS

As with many UFO sightings, no one will ever know for certain. But there are simple explanations for everything that happened:

1. Paragliders launch from the Mont Blanc massif before flying down to the town of Chamonix. The "giant wing" the climbers heard may have been a paraglider going past the ridge.

2. The flashing lights are likely to have been rays of sunlight reflecting from the wings of white-colored birds that fly above the Argentière glacier.

3. Another possibility is that the whole sighting is a **hoax**: the friends made it up as a way of getting publicity for their new business.

Glossary

abduction take someone away against their will

alien person or creature from elsewhere. In the context of UFOs, "alien" usually means beings from another planet.

allege say that something is true without offering proof

altitude height, usually height above sea level

analysis detailed examination

astronaut person who has been in space

atmosphere mood or feeling created by a place

atomic weight description of relative atomic mass

authorize allow or give permission for

axis central line around which a spinning globe moves.

balsa wood lightweight wood often used in craftwork for making models

chemical formula description of the chemicals that make up something. Water, for example, is described as H_2O.

clone exact copy of another living thing

console keyboard-type location that allows control of electronic devices

controversial something that causes a lot of argument

cylindrical round when viewed from its end and rectangular when viewed from the side

debris wreckage or garbage, usually left behind as the result of an accident

device tool or piece of equipment designed to be used for a particular purpose

diameter width of a circle at its widest point

evidence available facts and events that support a particular view or version of events

extraterrestrial creature from a world other than Earth

fake pretend, or a copy of something that is supposed to be mistaken for the original

flare device that burns to produce a bright light, usually to act as a warning

galaxy group of stars and heavenly bodies held together by gravity

hallucinogenic allowing people to enter a different state of mind, usually through the use of drugs. Often people are able to imagine things in this state of mind that they could not normally imagine.

hoax event that is faked, with the intention of fooling people into thinking it is real

intelligence officer member of the armed forces or security services involved in processing information, including some secret information

investigation formal inquiry to find out as much information as possible about something

investigator person who tries to discover the truth about an event

jettisoned thrown out, especially from a moving vehicle

massif compact group of mountain peaks

migrate concerning birds, when they fly away at a particular time of year to live in another region or climate

nuclear relating to the nucleus of an atom. Nuclear energy is energy that comes from splitting the nucleus of an atom.

outer space space outside Earth's atmosphere

propulsion force that moves an object. For example, rocket propulsion moves spacecraft using the force of rockets.

radar reflector device for reflecting electromagnetic radar waves

radioactive material made of atoms whose nuclei break down, giving off harmful radiation

residue what is left after something burns up or evaporates; anything that remains after the main part has been taken away

satellite spacecraft that is sent into orbit around Earth, the Moon, or another heavenly body.

Soviet describing something from the former USSR

spaceport place where spacecraft land and take off

theory possible explanation that has yet to be proved

tractor beam science-fiction idea in which a beam of energy is able to pull objects and people toward it

USSR Union of Soviet Socialist Republics, a communist country that has now broken up into several smaller countries

witness someone who sees an event

wreckage damaged parts of an object that have been broken in a crash or accident

Forensic Investigations

Forensics is a complex and fascinating business. Investigators working in various fields may be called upon to explain a past event or an ongoing situation that seems, at first, to be beyond explanation. Using scientific work methods and specialized equipment, investigators record and analyze all the information gathered. Sometimes answers present themselves quite easily, a manmade accident, event, or even a hoax, but occasionally years go by before any firm conclusions can be reached—if ever.

Criminal scientific investigators, known as forensic investigators, have to obtain evidence that can be used in a court of law. Investigators may be called upon to make identifications from DNA fragments, take fingerprints from a crime scene, check photographs for fakes, examine paper fibers under an electron microscope, find the age of ancient bones using radiocarbon dating, match tire tracks left by a getaway car, or compare known dental records to the corpse of an unknown person.

One person alone cannot master such a wide range of skills, and those involved in forensic investigations often perform highly specialized tasks. Ballistics experts, for example, will match projectiles with weapons and detect traces of explosives on fabric or skin. Toxicologists may be called on by a pathologist carrying out an autopsy to examine a particular organ for indications of a hard-to-detect poison.

In their way of working, all forensic investigators are scientific or medical professionals. In fact, the range of skills required is so broad it covers almost every aspect of science and medicine: physics, chemistry, biology, medicine and dentistry, anthropology, archaeology, and psychology. So any reader wanting to pursue a career in forensics will need to begin with an interest in science.

Useful Websites

A website that gives details of the criminal mind and the methods they use:
    http://www.crimelibrary.com/index.html

A site that gives detailed articles about various crime scene investigator techniques and tools:
    http://www.crime-scene-investigator.net/

The FBI's website for young adults:
    http://www.fbi.gov/kids/6th12th/6th12th.htm

A website detailing alien and UFO sightings:
    http://www.alien-ufos.com/

Further Reading

Innes, Brian. *Alien Visitors and Abductions.* Chicago: Raintree, 1998.

Innes, Brian. *Forensic Science.* Broomall, Penn.: Mason Crest Publishers, 2002.

Innes, Brian. *The Mysteries of UFOs.* Chicago: Raintree, 1998.

Oxlade, Chris. *The Mystery of Life on Other Planets.* Chicago: Heinemann Library, 2002.

Oxlade, Chris. *The Mystery of UFOs.* Chicago: Heinemann Library, 1999.

Pentland, Peter and Pennie Stoyles. *Forensic Science.* Broomall, Penn.: Chelsea House Publishers, 2003.

Index